HEALING POWER!

7 Supernatural Methods God Uses For You To Receive Healing

By Randy Clark

HEALING POWER!
7 Supernatural Methods God Uses For You To Receive Healing

©2015 RANDY CLARK
ISBN: 978-1-7324247-1-5

All rights reserved. No part of this book may be reproduced in any form or by any electronic or mechanical means, including information storage and retrieval systems, without written permission from the author, except in the case of a reviewer, who may quote brief passages embodied in critical articles or in a review.

Unless otherwise noted, all Scripture quotations are taken from the Holy Bible, New Living Translation, Copyright ©1996. Used by permission of Tyndale House Publishers, Inc., Wheaton, Illinois 60189. All rights reserved.

Scripture quotations marked (NKJV) are taken from the New King James Version® of the Bible. Copyright ©1982 by Thomas Nelson Inc.: Nashville. Used by permission. All rights reserved.

Underlining in Scripture quotations indicates the author's emphasis.

For more information about the author, visit his website:

www.RandyClark.info

Contents

Chapter 1: Is Healing For Today? 1

Chapter 2: Gift of Healing 9

Chapter 3: Prayer From Elders 19

Chapter 4: Laying On Of Hands 27

Chapter 5: Special Anointings 37

Chapter 6: Prayer Of Agreement 47

Chapter 7: Commanding Healing 57

Chapter 8: Believing God's Word 67

Chapter 9: Final Thoughts 77

About the Author 83

Chapter 1
Is Healing For Today?

Is God still willing to supernaturally heal people today or are those days long gone? That is a question many people have struggled with when confronted with a serious illness. Very few people doubt <u>God's ability to heal</u>. The main question folks have is whether <u>God wants to heal in today's world</u>. Or more specifically, does God want to heal me (or the person I am praying for) right now?

If you can get to the place that you believe God can and will still heal you or the person you are praying for, the next question is "How do I receive healing?" Do I have to read a certain prayer? Do I have to pray for several hours a day, begging God to help me? Do I have to call for a clergyman to read specific prayers over me? Do I have to find a "faith healer" to heal me?

I will briefly deal with the question of whether God still heals today in this first chapter. The rest of this book will describe the various ways described in the Bible that we can receive healing from God. One of the biggest hindrances to receiving healing is thinking that God only heals in one fashion. We will look at seven ways to receive healing from God. There are probably more than seven ways, but getting a revelation of these seven will help you get started in your understanding of healing.

Where Does Sickness Come From?

We don't live in heaven. We live on an earth that has been corrupted by sin. When God created the earth, He did not include sickness or disease or heartache. But, when mankind sinned, things changed. Adam and Eve gave in to the first sinner, Satan, and sin corrupted God's original creation. Murder and lying and

Chapter 1: Is Healing for Today?

sickness soon followed. Satan is the instigator of everything evil. Jesus made a statement that very clearly defines the difference between Satan, who is the thief, and Jesus.

The thief's purpose is to steal and kill and destroy. My purpose is to give them a rich and satisfying life. (John 10:10)

Sickness comes to <u>steal</u> your money by making you pay for doctors, medicine, rehabilitation, etc. Sickness comes to <u>kill</u> you if it continues to its final conclusion without intervention. Sickness comes to <u>destroy</u> your quality of life by limiting you or causing you pain. Jesus, however, came to bring you a full, complete and satisfying life without the constraints of sickness.

Peter, one of Jesus' most devoted followers and a leader in the development of the church, preached a powerful sermon one day. Look at part of what Peter said in that sermon about Jesus.

And you know that God anointed Jesus of Nazareth with the Holy Spirit and with

power. Then Jesus went around doing good and healing all who were oppressed by the devil, for God was with him. (Acts 10:38)

Notice that Jesus was "doing good and healing." Healing is a good thing. Sickness is a bad thing. Jesus was anointed with Holy Spirit power and demonstrated healing as part of the goodness of God. Also notice that Jesus healed "all who were oppressed by the devil." Once again, sickness originally came into the earth because of the devil. In that sense, sickness is part of the devil's oppression. Jesus delivered people from the devil's oppression of sickness. And finally, notice that "God was with Him." If healing wasn't God's will, Jesus would have been fighting against God by bringing healing to so many that He met. But God was working <u>with</u> Jesus to demonstrate His will of healing.

God's Will

While Jesus walked on the earth, He constantly demonstrated the will of God. Jesus al-

CHAPTER 1: IS HEALING FOR TODAY?

ways did what God, His Father, wanted Him to do. Jesus never disobeyed His Father. This is what Jesus said about His commitment to demonstrating God's will on the earth.

For I have come down from heaven to do the will of God who sent me, not to do my own will. (John 6:38)

Jesus demonstrated God's will as He healed all kinds of sickness. You may think there are new diseases that are too hard for God to heal. That isn't true. God's power is infinite. He can heal any kind of disease found in the earth now, or anytime in the future, just like He healed every disease he encountered in Bible days.

Jesus traveled throughout the region of Galilee, teaching in the synagogues and announcing the Good News about the Kingdom. <u>And he healed every kind of disease and illness</u>. (Matthew 4:23)

But Jesus knew what they were planning. So he left that area, and many people followed *him. <u>He healed all the sick among them</u>, (Matthew 12:15)*

As the sun went down that evening, people throughout the village brought sick family members to Jesus. <u>No matter what their diseases were, the touch of his hand healed every one.</u> (Luke 4:40)

Jesus never turned people away by telling them He did not want to heal them. But, did anyone ever ask Jesus if it was His will to heal? Yes, there was a man with leprosy who came to Jesus and asked Him the same kind of question we have been discussing. This man told Jesus he knew He <u>could</u> heal him. But his question was, did Jesus <u>want</u> to heal him. Look at this encounter and how Jesus responded.

A man with leprosy came and knelt in front of Jesus, begging to be healed. "If you are willing, you can heal me and make me clean," he said. Moved with compassion, Jesus reached out and touched him. "I am

Chapter 1: Is Healing for Today?

willing," he said. "Be healed!" Instantly the leprosy disappeared, and the man was healed. (Mark 1:40–42)

You may say that all those events happened thousands of years ago and just aren't relevant today. That would be inaccurate. Jesus hasn't changed, even though it has been a long time since He physically walked on the earth.

Jesus Christ is the same yesterday, today, and forever. (Hebrews 13:8)

Jesus didn't stop healing when He ascended back into Heaven. Thirty years after Jesus' resurrection, Jesus demonstrated His healing power through one of His disciples. Paul, an individual who began his commitment to Jesus after the resurrection, took the opportunity to deliver Jesus' healing power to a group of people on the island of Malta.

As it happened, Publius's father was ill with fever and dysentery. Paul went in and prayed for him, and laying his hands on him, he healed him. Then all the other sick people on the island came and were healed. (Acts 28:8–9)

Now it's time to look at seven ways that God provides His healing power to deliver people from the oppression of sickness.

Chapter 2
Gift of Healing

THE FIRST HEALING METHOD WE WILL DEscribe is the one most people have heard about. Unfortunately, many people who are familiar with this method of healing consider it to be fake. That is a sad commentary because this is truly a means that God still uses today to deliver His healing power. Just because some false ministers have used this as a way to obtain money or notoriety doesn't mean it isn't real. A counterfeit version of anything is only possible if there is also a legitimate version. So let's take a look at the details of this supernatural gift.

First of all, it is important to realize that the gift of healing is a supernatural gift. That means it is something that occurs outside the natural realm of events. It is supernatural because it comes from God, the Holy Spirit. God gave Paul a unique understanding of several supernatural gifts and how they operate. As the Holy Spirit revealed these things to Paul, he wrote them down in a letter to the Christian believers in the city of Corinth.

There are different kinds of spiritual gifts, but the same Spirit is the source of them all. There are different kinds of service, but we serve the same Lord. God works in different ways, but it is the same God who does the work in all of us. A spiritual gift is given to each of us so we can help each other. (1 Corinthians 12:4–7)

Notice that the Holy Spirit is the source of all the gifts. That means the Holy Spirit is the source of the gift of healing. Nobody owns the gift of healing because it belongs to the Holy Spirit. That means nobody can turn the gift of healing on and off at will. That is probably one of the most misunderstood things about

Chapter 2: Gift of Healing

this gift. Sceptics would say, "If you believe in healing, why don't you go heal everyone in the hospital?" If a person owned the gift and could turn it on and off at will, then I would say the same thing. However, that is not how it works. Verse 7 in another translation makes it more clear.

But the manifestation of the Spirit is given to each one for the profit of all: (1 Corinthians 12:7)(NKJV)

The gifts are all "manifestations" of the Holy Spirit. That means they are different ways that God demonstrates His goodness and mercy outside of the normal course of events. And it means that God determines when these manifestations occur. We can't make them happen whenever we want.

Also, notice that the purpose of the gift is to profit, or help others. The reason for the manifestation of supernatural healing is not to make someone famous or rich. The purpose of the gift of healing is to alleviate sickness in an individual, restore that person to health and demonstrate the goodness of God.

The same Spirit gives great faith to another, and to someone else the <u>one Spirit gives the gift of healing</u>. (1 Corinthians 12:9)

The Holy Spirit gives this gift to whomever He pleases. The gift isn't permanent. It works through an individual whenever the Holy Spirit wants it to work. We can ask for the gift to be manifested through us because God wants us to desire that His gifts would operate through us.

Pursue love, and desire spiritual gifts... (1 Corinthians 14:1)(NKJV)

But we can't make it work whenever we want. Even Jesus didn't make it work all the time. He encountered a lot of people during His ministry on the earth. However, He didn't heal everyone who needed healing. Look at this story about a time Jesus went to a certain place in Jerusalem called the pool of Bethesda. Apparently, people believed that an angel would come by occasionally and stir up the water in the pool. The people believed that whoever got in the pool first after the angel stirred the water would be healed. That is why the area around the pool was full of crowds of sick people who were looking for a way to be healed.

Afterward Jesus returned to Jerusalem for one of the Jewish holy days. Inside the city, near the Sheep Gate, was the pool of Bethesda, with five covered porches. Crowds of sick people—blind, lame, or paralyzed—lay on the porches. One of the men lying there had been sick for thirty-eight years. When Jesus saw him and knew he had been ill for a long time, he asked him, "Would you like to get well?" "I can't, sir," the sick man said, "for I have no one to put me into the pool when the water bubbles up. Someone else always gets there ahead of me." Jesus told him, "Stand up, pick up your mat, and walk!" Instantly, the man was healed! He rolled up his sleeping mat and began walking! ... (John 5:1–9)

There are several things to pay attention to in this story. First, this was a large area with five porches all around the pool to accommodate the crowds of sick people. That means a lot of sick people who needed to be healed were in this area around the pool. Second, the man Jesus targeted had been sick for 38 long years. It seems likely that a lot of the other people there had been sick for a long time, too.

Is Faith Required?

We established that this method of healing is manifested at God's direction. The third thing to consider is that we can't activate it with our faith. If you receive healing from God in this manner, it is simply a gift from God. A gift can't be earned. It can only be received or rejected. The only thing you can do to position yourself to receive healing this way is to be in the presence of someone through whom the Holy Spirit is manifesting this gift. Then you can be available and in place if God chooses to heal you through the gift of healing.

CHAPTER 2: GIFT OF HEALING

The story we are looking at is a good example of the operation of the gift of healing through Jesus. The man who had been ill for 38 years demonstrated no faith at all in Jesus' ability to heal him. Notice that when Jesus asked him if he wanted to be healed, the man immediately began to make excuses about why he couldn't get in the pool fast enough. Apparently, he knew nothing about Jesus. Jesus spoke to the man and told him to be healed. The gift of healing was manifested and the man stood up and began to walk; something he had not done in 38 years.

Only One

The fourth thing we can observe from this story is that only one of the many folks needing healing was healed by the gift of healing. God's power is unlimited, and He certainly could have manifested the gift of healing to restore everybody in the large crowd to health. But He didn't. Why? Some things we don't know "why." We just know at this particular time, in the sovereignty of God, He only chose to heal one person through a manifestation of the gift of healing. That doesn't mean He didn't heal any of the crowd at a later time. That doesn't mean Jesus didn't love all those people. It just means that sometimes God makes decisions we may not understand. If you have gone to a meeting where an evangelist operated in the gift of healing and you didn't get healed, please don't be discouraged. That is only one way God manifests healing. Just because He didn't heal you through the gift of healing on that day doesn't mean you will never get well. Maybe your day is coming with a different method of healing.

Has The Gift Of Healing Expired?

Maybe you have wondered if the gift of healing is still even an option for today. Some folks take the position that the gift of healing was only for Jesus while he was physically on the earth or just to help Christianity spread in

CHAPTER 2: GIFT OF HEALING

the early days described in the Bible. A certain segment of believers would say that the gift has already served its purpose and has ended. I don't believe that is what the word of God teaches in the Bible. When used in the Bible, the word "church" refers to all believers in Jesus, both those still living on earth and those already in heaven. As long as there are believers on the earth, the church is still around. As Paul was inspired by the Holy Spirit to teach about the gifts of the Holy Spirit, he explained that the gifts are to operate through believers, the church. So as long as the church is here, the gifts are still operational.

Here are some of the parts <u>God has appointed for the church</u>: first are apostles, second are prophets, third are teachers, then those who do miracles, <u>those who have the gift of healing</u>, those who can help others, those who have the gift of leadership, those who speak in unknown languages. (1 Corinthians 12:28)

The gift of healing is a wonderful blessing from the hand of God. We should celebrate and thank Him when this gift is used to bring healing and restoration to those who are suffering. This is <u>one</u> way that God heals. But it isn't the <u>only</u> way.

Chapter 3
Prayer From Elders

SICKNESS CAN MAKE A PERSON WEAK. PHYSIcally weak because the body is using a great deal of energy to fight against the sickness. Emotionally weak because of the distraction from your daily affairs and, many times, fear caused by wondering if and when you will get well. Spiritually weak because of the energy you expend to pray and believe that God will somehow make a way for you to recover from your illness. Sometimes the reputation of the sickness to cause great harm, or even death, can overwhelm you.

In times like this, you need help. You shouldn't have to face those challenges alone. You should call out for help. The Bible gives specific instructions for times where you feel overmatched in your resistance to sickness.

Are any of you suffering hardships? You should pray.... (James 5:13)

Whenever you face hard times, the first reaction should be to call out to God for help. Sometimes we are too quick to cry out to others to pray for us. Before you ask anyone else to pray for you, you should go to God yourself and ask Him for help. Regardless of whether your hardship is sickness, discouragement, financial distress, confusion or anything else, you need to go to the source of all wisdom, the Holy Spirit, and ask Him what to do. He promised he would give you His wisdom.

If you need wisdom, ask our generous God, and he will give it to you. He will not rebuke you for asking. (James 1:5)

Ask God if there is anything you did to cause the sickness with which you are dealing. Maybe something in your diet is causing the problem. Maybe you are stressed and not sleeping well and, as a result, your immune

Chapter 3: Prayer From Elders

system is weakened. Maybe you have an infection and can easily get well by taking a round of antibiotics. There are a lot of reasons you can be sick, so ask God for His wisdom before taking any action. If the sickness remains, the next step is to ask for help from your brothers and sisters in the church.

Are any of you sick? You should call for the elders of the church to come and pray over you, anointing you with oil in the name of the Lord. (James 5:14)

The second method for receiving healing we will look at is described in the verse above. Calling for the elders of the church.

So, who are the elders? The word "elder" comes from the Greek word "presbyterous," which refers to pastors and ministers. Those individuals are in a position of spiritual responsibility. The elders are spiritually mature. They have developed their faith and have learned to trust and depend on God to help them in times of need.

They are also described as "elders of the church." The Greek word translated "church" is "ekklesias." That refers to all people who have responded to Jesus by putting their trust in Him for their salvation. There are thousands of local church groups in the world. You will find the spiritually mature, faith-filled ministers you need in a local church. You should be a faithful member of a local church. According to the Bible, one of the responsibilities of the pastors and ministers in the church is to pray for the sick when called upon.

Consider what you would do if you had a large piano that you needed to move. The piano weighs too much for you to lift by yourself. The size of the piano makes it impossible for you to get a good grip even if you could lift the weight by yourself. So what can you do to get the piano where you need it to be? You could find five others who would help you with your project. None of you by yourself could lift the piano. But, if you all surround the piano and lift together at the same time, you can much more easily get the piano where you want it moved.

The same principal applies when you face a sickness that has become more than you can handle on your own. The elders are strong in faith. They should be willing to join with you to help remove the sickness that has become a heavy burden in your life. Perhaps if several elders gather with you and join their faith together, the combined faith of all of you will be enough to lift the sickness off of you.

Anointing With Oil

This passage of Scripture also instructs the elders to anoint the sick with oil. Oil is used in numerous places in the Bible to signify the Holy Spirit. The oil itself is not what will bring healing to a person. The oil is representative of the healing God manifests through the power of the Holy Spirit. The type of oil used is irrelevant. It doesn't have to be oil from the Holy Land. It can be vegetable oil, fragrant oil, olive oil or some other type. The healing power comes from Him who is symbolized by the oil. Always remember it is God's healing power we are seeking. The important thing to recognize is that when you feel the oil on your skin, it represents the Holy Spirit power you are seeking for your freedom from sickness. The early church disciples had success by using this method of healing.

So the disciples went out, telling everyone they met to repent of their sins and turn to God. And they cast out many demons and healed many sick people, anointing them with olive oil. (Mark 6:12–13)

Begin To Believe

When you are anointed with oil, that also gives you and the elders a place and time to release your faith and begin to believe together for a manifestation of healing. Much like the start of a race is the time to push off with your feet and begin to run down the track. The prayer of the elders gives you all a point in time to activate your faith. It can be a time to start believing and trusting for God to do a mighty work to provide His healing power to restore you to health.

The Name Of The Lord

The instructions in the Scripture are for the elders to pray "in the name of the Lord." So what is the name of the Lord? His name is "Jesus!" Jesus is God, manifested in human form. God (the Father), Jesus (the Son), and the Holy Spirit are what many refer to as the "Trinity." The name of Jesus represents everything He is and everything He can do. If the elders don't believe in the authority and power of the name of Jesus, their prayers will likely do you no good.

Such a prayer offered in faith will heal the sick, and the Lord will make you well. (James 5:15)

Elders must also believe in healing or there is no faith. Once again, you are wasting your time if the elders believe healing stopped when the original apostles died; or if they believe God only heals through medical science now.

But also notice that "the Lord will make you well." We ultimately look to Jesus as the healer, even though we ask the elders to follow God's instructions by anointing with oil, praying in Jesus' name and praying a believing prayer.

I thank God that He is still manifesting healing today as a result of the prayers of elders. We should celebrate and thank Him when this method is used to bring healing and restoration to those who are suffering. This is <u>one</u> way that God heals. But it isn't the <u>only</u> way.

Chapter 4
Laying On Of Hands

JESUS ISSUED AN AMAZING DIRECTIVE SHORTly before He left the earth and ascended back to heaven. Miracles and healing had been a part of the ministry of Jesus for over three years. Multitudes of people followed Jesus, hoping to receive supernatural healing or witness Jesus heal someone. On this day He revealed that miracle signs would continue to be manifested on the earth even after He was no longer physically walking the earth. Jesus declared that demonstrating miraculous signs would be part of the ministry of His followers. And one of the signs He described was that believers would be able to carry God's healing power to sick people.

These miraculous signs will accompany those who believe: They will cast out demons in my name, and they will speak in new languages. They will be able to handle snakes with safety, and if they drink anything poisonous, it won't hurt them. They will be able to place their hands on the sick, and they will be healed." (Mark 16:17–18)

Since this book is about healing, I am going to focus on the part in Jesus' command concerning healing. The other parts mean other things and, because you may be curious, I will give a cursory explanation of the other commands.

Demons are real and believers have authority over demons because the blood of Jesus has cleansed us of our sins. Because Jesus sent back the Holy Spirit, He has provided a way for every believer to pray the perfect will of God directly to our heavenly Father in a supernatural language. Handling snakes is not a literal command, but a metaphor for dealing with demons through the authority of Jesus' name. Safety from drinking anything deadly isn't a

Chapter 4: Laying On Of Hands

command to test God by deliberately drinking poison. It just means if you have to drink something you are not sure about, especially in a foreign country, Jesus will protect you from harm.

Notice that Jesus said that these signs will follow "those who believe." Believe what? First of all, you must believe in Jesus as your Savior and Lord and the Son of God. These signs are not going to follow people who only believe that Jesus was a good teacher. Or people who only believe that Jesus was a good moral man who lived a really good life.

Second, you must believe that Jesus is still able and willing to heal people today. If you have bought into the notion that supernatural healing stopped thousands of years ago, you are wasting your time laying hands on sick people. It won't happen for you or the one for whom you're praying.

Third, you must believe that Jesus' name is more powerful than any sickness you can face. Consider what Jesus did while He was here in person. Many times when sick people came to

Him, Jesus healed them and restored them to health. Jesus wants His ministry of healing to continue, even though He is in heaven. And so Jesus delegated the authority to act on His behalf to believers. He told us that we could use His name to accomplish His will on the earth. He told us to use His name to deliver His healing power to those in need. Jesus' name is more powerful than the name of any sickness ever known.

Therefore, God elevated him to the place of highest honor and gave him the name above all other names, that at the name of Jesus every knee should bow, in heaven and on earth and under the earth, (Philippians 2:9–10)

Fourth, you must believe that God's supernatural healing power resides in your spirit and is available to flow out of you and into the person needing healing. That is a truth most Christians may have never really considered. The same powerful Holy Spirit who raised Jesus from the dead lives inside your physical body.

CHAPTER 4: LAYING ON OF HANDS

The Spirit of God, who raised Jesus from the dead, lives in you. And just as God raised Christ Jesus from the dead, he will give life to your mortal bodies by this same Spirit living within you. (Romans 8:11)

It's Elementary

People have different reactions when they hear someone talk about "laying on of hands." Some folks come from a very structured religious background where nobody has ever used that phrase at all. Others resist the notion totally because they consider such a thing as only being done by extreme groups operating on the fringe of truth. But what does the Bible say about it? Isn't that all that really matters if we want to know the truth?

So let us stop going over the <u>basic teachings about Christ</u> again and again. Let us go on instead and become mature in our understanding. Surely we don't need to start *again with the fundamental importance of repenting from evil deeds and placing our faith in God. You don't need further instruction about baptisms, <u>the laying on of hands</u>, the resurrection of the dead, and eternal judgment. And so, God willing, we will move forward to further understanding. (Hebrews 6:1–3)*

The writer of Hebrews tells us that we should be growing up and not having to be taught the basics over and over. This scripture describes some of the "basic teachings" about Jesus that we should learn when we first start to follow Him. This is similar to elementary school students being taught very basic knowledge about arithmetic, spelling, science etc. They don't teach calculus or physics in elementary school. They teach the foundational truths that need to be understood so that, as students progress in school, they can learn more advanced topics. So this scripture lists several truths that are considered "basic," or "elementary." And one of the items in the list

Chapter 4: Laying On Of Hands

is "the laying on of hands." Laying on of hands is one of the basic doctrines of Christ found in the Bible. It is used for ministering healing and the baptism of the Holy Spirit, setting individuals apart for ministry, casting out demons and delivering blessings.

Laying on of hands isn't something extreme. It isn't something to be feared. It isn't something that passed away thousands of years ago. It is a basic doctrine of Christ and should be embraced by all believers. It is one of the ways that Jesus uses to deliver His healing power to those in need.

Now that you are considering this method, you may wonder about how to do it. For example, where do I lay my hands? The Bible doesn't give any specific instructions. You don't have to necessarily put your hands on the part of the body that needs healing. In my experience, most of the time I have either put my hands on someone's head or shoulders. I have also taken a person's hand many times and prayed for them that way. You don't have to make a big scene when you lay hands on someone for healing. The key is believing and using the name of Jesus.

Praying More Than Once

I want to show you an example in the ministry of Jesus of how this works. Here's the story.

When they arrived at Bethsaida, some people brought a blind man to Jesus, and they begged him to <u>touch the man and heal him</u>. Jesus took the blind man by the hand and led him out of the village. Then, spitting on the man's eyes, <u>he laid his hands on him</u> and asked, "Can you see anything now?" The man looked around. "Yes," he said, "I see people, but I can't see them very clearly. They look like trees walking around." Then <u>Jesus placed his hands on the man's eyes again</u>, and his eyes were opened. His sight was completely restored, and he could see everything clearly. (Mark 8:22–25)

Chapter 4: Laying On Of Hands

Notice that the people took the initiative to take a blind man to Jesus. They knew that Jesus was the source for healing. You should always remember that also. Even though you are laying hands on someone or someone is laying hands on you, Jesus is the source for the healing you are seeking.

Also, notice that the people begged Jesus to touch the man. They had seen Jesus in operation before and they knew that healing power flowed out of Him when He touched people. Jesus took the man to a private place and spit on the man's eyes. Isn't that strange? Spitting on someone is normally a great insult. In Bible days, someone who was spit upon had to wash themselves and were considered unclean for a certain time. In this instance, Jesus was spitting on the blindness and expressing His contempt for the corruption of blindness that was in the earth because of Satan. There is nothing in the Bible, however, that commands us to spit on anyone.

Then Jesus laid His hands on the man and asked him if he could see. The man replied that he could discern people, but they were blurry and that his healing was not complete. Why did the man not receive his complete healing when Jesus first laid hands on him? Certainly Jesus was not at fault. The Bible doesn't say why, however, it does reveal that Jesus laid His hands on the man a second time.

Sometimes people hesitate to ask someone to lay hands on them a second time because they think it would demonstrate a lack of faith. Well, Jesus had no hesitation in laying hands on the man a second time. And the second time, the man was completely healed. So I encourage you to continue to take whatever steps you need to see your healing manifested.

I thank God that He is still manifesting healing today as a result of believers laying hands on the sick. We should celebrate and thank Him when this method is used to bring healing and restoration to those who are suffering. This is <u>one</u> way that God heals. But it isn't the <u>only</u> way.

Chapter 5
Special Anointings

SOMETIMES GOD DOES SOMETHING UNIQUE and special to bring healing to a person. Because He is infinite and He is the source of healing, He can manifest Himself any way He wants. Under this category, there are really no rules. I will focus on one unusual way that God healed with a special anointing. I want you to be familiar with it because He can still use this method today.

God gave Paul the power to perform unusual miracles. When handkerchiefs or aprons that had merely touched his skin were placed on sick people, they were healed of their diseases, and evil spirits were expelled. (Acts 19:11–12)

Notice that God is the one who gave this special power to Paul. Paul didn't do anything to earn it. God just did it as an act of His will. Also notice that He refers to this method as "unusual." That means it was not something that happened in the normal course of events. It appears that this power only manifested itself at certain times. Paul couldn't turn it on or turn it off at will.

And finally, notice that this power enabled Paul to do "unusual miracles." The word translated "miracles" is from the Greek word "dunamis," which is also translated as "power," "mighty work" and "strength." A miracle is an occurrence of God's mighty power and strength that happens outside the natural order of life and outside of the established laws of nature and science.

The word translated "handkerchief" is very clear. It is simply a cloth used in various ways such as wiping perspiration from the face. The word "apron" refers to a linen apron which workmen and servants used. In both cases, it is obvious the context refers to a type of cloth.

Chapter 5: Special Anointings

During these extraordinary times, cloths that had been in contact with Paul's body became saturated with the healing power of Jesus. This healing power was so strong that it remained in the cloths for a certain period of time. When they were placed on a sick person, the healing power of Jesus would flow out of the cloths into the sick person and cause them to be restored to health. The power of God would also drive out any demon spirits which were present.

So how could something like this happen? Remember that miracles occur outside the normal laws of nature. The healing power of God is a spiritual force which affects a person's physical body. A spiritual force, such as healing, is not something that can be physically measured like an electrical current. However, it is just as real as something you can perceive with your five physical senses.

The word "anointed" or "anointing" is a way of describing how God transfers His power to a person or thing. Jesus operated with this same powerful healing anointing. Jesus is

God, manifested in human form, and He never stopped being God. However, in order for Him to come into the earth as a human being, He willingly laid aside His powers of deity which came with being God.

You must have the same attitude that Christ Jesus had. Though he was God, he did not think of equality with God as something to cling to. Instead, <u>he gave up his divine privileges; he took the humble position of a slave and was born as a human being</u>. When he appeared in human form, he humbled himself in obedience to God and died a criminal's death on a cross. (Philippians 2:5–8)

Because Jesus laid aside His divine privileges to become a man, He needed the anointing of God to perform the healings and miracles that He performed. Peter, one of Jesus' disciples, describes this in a sermon he preached about Jesus one day in the home of a man named Cornelius.

CHAPTER 5: SPECIAL ANOINTINGS

And you know that God anointed Jesus of Nazareth with the Holy Spirit and with power. Then Jesus went around doing good and healing all who were oppressed by the devil, for God was with him. (Acts 10:38)

This healing anointing was manifested regularly as Jesus walked on the earth and delivered physical healing to those who were sick. Even though it is a spiritual force, it affects the human body and, in some cases, can even be felt with the physical senses. Look at this story about a woman who was in desperate need of healing. Jesus was headed to a man's house to heal the man's daughter when He was interrupted in a very unique way.

Jesus went with him, and all the people followed, crowding around him. A woman in the crowd had suffered for twelve years with constant bleeding. She had suffered a great deal from many doctors, and over the years she had spent everything she had to pay them, but she had gotten no better. In

41

fact, she had gotten worse. She had heard about Jesus, so she came up behind him through the crowd and <u>touched his robe</u>. For she thought to herself, "<u>If I can just touch his robe, I will be healed.</u>" Immediately the bleeding stopped, and she could feel in her body that she had been healed of her terrible condition. Jesus realized at once that <u>healing power had gone out from him</u>, so he turned around in the crowd and asked, "Who touched my robe?" His disciples said to him, "Look at this crowd pressing around you. How can you ask, 'Who touched me?'" But he kept on looking around to see who had done it. Then the frightened woman, trembling at the realization of what had happened to her, came and fell to her knees in front of him and told him what she had done. And he said to her, "Daughter, your faith has made you well. Go in peace. Your suffering is over." (Mark 5:24–34)

There are several things to note in this story. First of all, the woman only touched Jesus' robe. And when she touched His robe, she was immediately healed. Jesus' healing power, His healing anointing, saturated His robe, so that when the woman touched His robe in faith, she was healed. This is very similar to the special healing miracles which occurred when Paul was so saturated with God's healing power that the healing power transferred to the cloths which were in contact with his body.

Also, notice that both the woman and Jesus felt the healing power flowing from Jesus into the woman's sick body. Even though it is a spiritual force, it manifested itself physically to heal the woman's body. Jesus was in a huge crowd of people. Folks were jostling Him constantly as He walked through the crowd. But only one person who touched Him received healing. Why was that? Because the sick woman is the only one who touched Him with her faith. She believed that she would be healed when she touched Jesus' robe.

She had heard about Jesus performing healing miracles and she had made up her mind that she would be one who received one of those healing miracles. Jesus told her why she had been healed when He said to her, "your faith has made you well." Even though Jesus' healing anointing was available for everyone in the crowd, her faith is what drew that power out of Jesus and into her body.

After they had crossed the lake, they landed at Gennesaret. When the people recognized Jesus, the news of his arrival spread quickly throughout the whole area, and soon people were bringing all their sick to be healed. They begged him to let the sick touch at least the fringe of his robe, and all who touched him were healed. (Matthew 14:34–36)

Jesus' fame spread quickly. Many people who were sick realized that healing power flowed out of Jesus when people would believe. Everyone who touched even the fringe on Jesus' robe received the healing they were seeking. The healing anointing of Jesus flowed from Him on a regular basis. Huge crowds followed him realizing that God's healing power was available through Jesus.

When they came down from the mountain, the disciples stood with Jesus on a large, level area, surrounded by many of his followers and by the crowds. There were people from all over Judea and from Jerusalem and from as far north as the seacoasts of Tyre and Sidon. They had come to hear him and to be healed of their diseases; and those troubled by evil spirits were healed. Everyone tried to touch him, because healing power went out from him, and he healed everyone. (Luke 6:17–19)

The tangible, healing anointing of God is still flowing today. There is nothing in the Bible that says this method of healing has ceased. But remember, this is a unique way of delivering healing power when Jesus manifests His healing anointing in a special way. Nobody can purchase a healing from God by giving money to an individual for a prayer cloth.

I thank God that He is still manifesting healing today through special anointings. We should celebrate and thank Him when this method is used to bring healing and restoration to those who are suffering. This is <u>one</u> way that God heals. But it isn't the <u>only</u> way.

Chapter 6
Prayer Of Agreement

ONE DAY JESUS WAS IN THE CITY OF CAPERnaum answering questions from people and teaching some wonderful truths about God and how to live according to His principles. During this teaching session, Jesus made a very interesting statement about prayer that has an application for receiving healing from God. This is what Jesus said:

"I also tell you this: If two of you agree here on earth concerning anything you ask, my Father in heaven will do it for you. For where two or three gather together as my followers, I am there among them." (Matthew 18:19–20)

Jesus said this prayer principle applies to people on earth. That means this isn't something that only happens in heaven. This prayer works now, while we are all still on the earth. And since it works for us now, we should take the time to understand what Jesus is talking about.

Next, Jesus said two people have to agree about the prayer request. In looking at numerous modern dictionaries, the word "agree" is a verb described as meaning: *To share an opinion or feeling; be in accord. To express consent; concur. To decide something together.*

The actual Greek word in the Bible which is translated "agree" is "**sumphōneō**," which means: *to call out with, to be in harmony.* This Greek word comes from the root word, "**sumphōnia**," which means: *symphony,* i.e. *music.*

Jesus places very high importance on the "agreement" part of praying and asking for something from God, our Father. Agreement seems to be the key to the prayer being heard and answered. As we saw from the Greek word definitions, the two people praying have to be

Chapter 6: Prayer of Agreement

"in harmony" together. When two people are singing together and harmonizing together, they both have to be singing in the same key. They both have to be singing with the same tempo. They both have to be singing the same words. There is a lot to agree on if you are going to sing in harmony.

The Greek root word definition for "agree" refers to a "symphony." There are even more things to agree on for an orchestra to perform a symphony. It takes all the musicians playing their instruments "in one accord." They each have to agree to follow the lead of the orchestra conductor. They have to start at exactly the same time and end together. Just like the singers singing in harmony, they all must agree on the tempo of the music. A symphony orchestra would be a disaster if the musicians each decided to play a different piece of music instead of agreeing to play the music selected by the conductor.

These same principles apply to joining in prayer with one or more people to ask God to heal you or someone else. In order to be in agreement for a healing request, several questions come to mind that have to be addressed. First, do both of you believe Jesus is still healing today? Many people don't believe that supernatural healing is still something that God does anymore. Some folks think that healing was just for the early church to get started and that it passed away after the first 12 apostles died. Nothing in the Bible says that, but many people have that opinion. There is no need to pray with someone who doesn't believe God will answer a prayer request for healing. You wouldn't be in agreement and this method of receiving healing would not work.

A second question that comes to mind is, do both of you believe God wants to heal the person for whom you are praying? Some people think God punishes people for their sins with sickness and that they deserve to be sick. The Bible says in **Romans 3:23** that we have all sinned. So if that were the case, we would all deserve to be sick because of our sin. The truth of the gospel is that Jesus paid the penal-

Chapter 6: Prayer of Agreement

ty for our sins so we won't have to suffer the consequences. I believe people should live a sanctified life and stay away from sin. However, in Bible days, Jesus healed a lot of people and there is no record of Him ever refusing to heal someone because of their sin. Many times Jesus heals as an act of His grace, which is his unmerited favor.

Another aspect of this second question is that some people believe God sends or allows sickness to teach us things. God can teach you things in any circumstance you find yourself. Just because you learned something during a difficult time doesn't mean God caused it or allowed it for His purpose.

Many years ago, I had a friend whose wife was in the hospital. I asked my friend if I could pray for his wife to be healed and he said, "No, I would rather you wouldn't do that." When I asked him why he didn't want me to pray, he said that it might not be God's will for her to get well. This man had his wife in the hospital under a doctor's care and the doctor was trying to help her get well. But her husband told me not to pray for her because it might not be God's will to heal her.

So which is it? Do you want her well or not? If it isn't God's will, then aren't you fighting against God by taking her to a doctor to try to get her well? If one person thinks God wants the person sick for a reason, you won't be in agreement and you need not even pray about it.

The key to operating in this healing prayer principle is to find a place where you can agree. Let me give you some examples of how to do this.

If a person is very sick and planning on a surgical procedure to correct the problem and you want to pray for a miraculous healing so that person won't need surgery, the two of you are not in agreement. You should realize that God can work through medical science to help a person get well. So the way to get into agreement in this case would be for both of you to agree that God will protect the sick

Chapter 6: Prayer of Agreement

person during the surgery, guide the hands of the surgeon and enable the patient to have a speedy recovery. If you do that, you are both in agreement and God can respond to the faith of both people.

This method of healing can work in conjunction with laying hands on people. Remember that Jesus said in Mark 16:17–18 that believers *"will lay hands on the sick, and they will recover."(NKJV)* Before you lay hands on someone to believe for healing, you should ask what they are believing for. That will help you get into agreement instead of assuming you know and praying a prayer that the sick person does not believe will ever be answered. You need to find out what they want in order to locate a place of agreement. Jesus followed this principle when He delivered healing to two blind men one day.

After Jesus left the girl's home, two blind men followed along behind him, shouting, "Son of David, have mercy on us!" They went right into the house where he was staying, and Jesus asked them, "Do you believe I can make you see?" "Yes, Lord," they told him, "we do." Then he touched their eyes and said, "Because of your faith, it will happen." (Matthew 9:27–30)

Notice that Jesus asked the men what they believed. He wanted to make sure they agreed with Him. Once He located their faith, Jesus got in agreement with them and delivered what they were believing for.

This agreement principle works for more than two people. In the first Scripture passage we looked at, Jesus goes on to say that, *"where two or three gather together as my followers, I am there among them."* Jesus had previously stated the importance of being in agreement. Then he made this statement. What Jesus was saying was that when two or more people will pray in agreement about a need, He will be there among them to cause that prayer to be answered. That is why it is important in larger prayer gatherings for everyone to be in agreement. One of the best ways to be in agreement in prayer is to pray the word of God. When you find promises in the Bible and pray them back to God, you know you are praying the will of God and you can all be in agreement.

I thank God that He is still manifesting healing today through the prayer of agreement. We should celebrate and thank Him when this method is used to bring healing and restoration to those who are suffering. This is <u>one</u> way that God heals. But it isn't the <u>only</u> way.

Chapter 7

Commanding Healing

GOD'S WORDS CARRY GREAT POWER. GOD created the heavens and the earth by speaking them into existence. Genesis 1:27 says, *"So God created human beings in his own image."* Because we are created in His image, our words also have the potential of carrying great power. We don't have the capacity to create a universe in the way that God did it. However, when our words are anointed and empowered by the Holy Spirit, great things can happen. Speaking commands is one way we can exercise our faith. Let's look at a story that illustrates this truth about speaking and commanding as a demonstration of your faith.

The next morning as they were leaving Bethany, Jesus was hungry. He noticed a fig tree in full leaf a little way off, so he went over to see if he could find any figs. But there were only leaves because it was too early in the season for fruit. Then Jesus said to the tree, "May no one ever eat your fruit again!" And the disciples heard him say it. (Mark 11:12–14)

Jesus did something that was very unusual. He spoke to a tree! Jesus apparently spoke loudly because *"the disciples heard Him say it."* That isn't something they had ever seen before. But Jesus was teaching them about one aspect of living by faith in God and His delegated authority. Maybe the disciples didn't think too much about it right when it happened. But the next morning something about that fig tree got their attention.

The next morning as they passed by the fig tree he had cursed, the disciples noticed it had withered from the roots up. Peter remembered what Jesus had said to the tree on the previous day and exclaimed, "Look,

Chapter 7: Commanding Healing

Rabbi! The fig tree you cursed has withered and died!" Then Jesus said to the disciples, "Have faith in God. I tell you the truth, you can say to this mountain, 'May you be lifted up and thrown into the sea,' and it will happen. But you must really believe it will happen and have no doubt in your heart. (Mark 11:20–23)

The fig tree that Jesus spoke to had died! Apparently, the roots had died the moment Jesus spoke to the tree and said it would never bear fruit again. Since the roots died, the rest of the tree withered away since no more life was being produced in the roots.

Then Jesus took the opportunity to teach His disciples a principle about living by faith. Jesus said that speaking and commanding are both one aspect of exercising your faith. He used the metaphor of a mountain and said you can speak to the mountain and command it to be moved out of your way. Jesus is describing any mountain, or obstacle, that is in your way and hindering you from fulfilling the will of

God in your life. He said you should exercise your faith by speaking to that mountain of adversity and commanding it to be removed. That may not be all you have to do for victory over that obstacle, but it is one aspect of exercising your faith in God.

Jesus demonstrated the power of commanding healing when He encountered a man who needed healing from leprosy. Notice how Jesus used two healing methods to deliver healing to this man. He touched him and He spoke healing to him.

A man with leprosy came and knelt in front of Jesus, begging to be healed. "If you are willing, you can heal me and make me clean," he said. Moved with compassion, Jesus reached out and touched him. "I am willing," he said. "Be healed!" Instantly the leprosy disappeared, and the man was healed. (Mark 1:40–42)

Jesus delivered the healing power of God when He spoke and told the man to *"Be*

CHAPTER 7: COMMANDING HEALING

healed!" The healing power of God drove out the sickness of leprosy and delivered healing to this man who had asked for a healing miracle from Jesus.

Jesus had another unusual encounter with someone needing healing when He was in the city of Capernaum. Jesus had become very well-known because of His healing miracles. As a result, hordes of people followed Him, hoping to either receive healing or witness a miracle.

When Jesus returned to Capernaum several days later, the news spread quickly that he was back home. Soon the house where he was staying was so packed with visitors that there was no more room, even outside the door. While he was preaching God's word to them, four men arrived carrying a paralyzed man on a mat. They couldn't bring him to Jesus because of the crowd, so they dug a hole through the roof above his head. Then they lowered the man on his mat, right down in front of Jesus. (Mark 2:1–4)

A paralyzed man was intent on getting to Jesus so he could be healed. When four friends of the paralyzed man arrived at the house, the crowd was so large there was no way to get inside. The men would not be deterred. They were convinced that if they could get their friend in front of Jesus he would be healed. They went to extreme measures to get their friend in the room with the Healer. After a short discussion with some of the religious leaders in the room about Jesus' ability to forgive sins, Jesus took action.

...Then Jesus turned to the paralyzed man and said, "Stand up, pick up your mat, and go home!" And the man jumped up, grabbed his mat, and walked out through the stunned onlookers. They were all amazed and praised God, exclaiming, "We've never seen anything like this before!" (Mark 2:10–12)

Jesus told the man to do something that seemed impossible. He told him to stand up and walk home! How can a paralyzed man stand up and walk home? Only if the paraly-

Chapter 7: Commanding Healing

sis is healed! By telling the man to stand up and walk, Jesus was commanding the man to be healed. The man obeyed Jesus and did something that seemed impossible just a few minutes before. Healing was manifested when Jesus spoke words of faith and authority.

This method of commanding healing continued after Jesus ascended back into heaven. Two of Jesus' disciples demonstrated this means of delivering healing one afternoon when a man who had been crippled since he was born cried out for help.

Peter and John went to the Temple one afternoon to take part in the three o'clock prayer service. As they approached the Temple, a man lame from birth was being carried in. Each day he was put beside the Temple gate, the one called the Beautiful Gate, so he could beg from the people going into the Temple. When he saw Peter and John about to enter, he asked them for some money. Peter and John looked at him intently, and Peter said, "Look at us!" The lame man looked at them eagerly, expecting some money. But Peter said, "I don't have any silver or gold for you. But I'll give you what I have. In the name of Jesus Christ the Nazarene, get up and walk!" Then Peter took the lame man by the right hand and helped him up. And as he did, the man's feet and ankles were instantly healed and strengthened. He jumped up, stood on his feet, and began to walk! Then, walking, leaping, and praising God, he went into the Temple with them. All the people saw him walking and heard him praising God. (Acts 3:1–9)

This man spent every afternoon in front of the temple asking for money. The beggar was calling out for anyone to help him and give him some money. He probably didn't focus on anyone in particular, he just cried out for help as people were walking by on the way into the temple. Peter and John were regular visitors to the temple, but something caused them to stop and pay attention to this beggar that day. Peter told him he wasn't going to give him any

Chapter 7: Commanding Healing

money that day. But he gave him something much more valuable than money. He spoke to the man with the authority of Jesus. Peter commanded the man to stand up and walk. Now, how can a man who has been lame since he was born stand up and walk? Only if he is healed by the power of God! Peter reached out and helped the man do something he had never done before. The crippled man began to rise and as he did, his healing was manifested and he began to walk.

When you want to use this method of healing, begin to speak and command healing to come and sickness to go. Don't be afraid to command healing in your body or the person for whom you are praying. Tell the sickness to leave and speak healing and restoration. Believe in your heart that your words carry healing power. And expect the best by believing in your heart that God's healing power is working.

I thank God that He is still manifesting healing today through believers who are commanding healing. We should celebrate and thank Him when this method is used to bring healing and restoration to those who are suffering. This is <u>one</u> way that God heals. But it isn't the <u>only</u> way.

Chapter 8
Believing God's Word

THE FINAL METHOD WE WILL CONSIDER FOR receiving supernatural healing from God is one that involves using your own faith to believe for what you need. Jesus was a perfect man and walked in perfect faith. None of us can match His perfection and His 100% success rate, but we can do our best to believe and trust God to deliver His healing power as a result of our faith. Let's start out by looking at a story of a man who walked in an extraordinary level of faith. It was faith of such a high order that Jesus took special note of it.

When Jesus returned to Capernaum, a Roman officer came and pleaded with him, "Lord, my young servant lies in bed, para-

lyzed and in terrible pain." Jesus said, "I will come and heal him." But the officer said, "Lord, I am not worthy to have you come into my home. Just say the word from where you are, and my servant will be healed. I know this because I am under the authority of my superior officers, and I have authority over my soldiers. I only need to say, 'Go,' and they go, or 'Come,' and they come. And if I say to my slaves, 'Do this,' they do it." When Jesus heard this, he was amazed. Turning to those who were following him, he said, "I tell you the truth, I haven't seen faith like this in all Israel! (Matthew 8:5–10)

The Roman officer sought out Jesus because he had a specific healing request. If you need healing for yourself or someone else, you should also approach Jesus with a very specific request for healing. The Roman described the condition of his servant and Jesus immediately agreed to go and heal him. But then the officer said something that set him apart from most people who approached Jesus for healing. The

Chapter 8: Believing God's Word

Roman told Jesus he understood the authority and power of Jesus' words. The officer said if Jesus would just speak healing, it would happen. This is very similar to the "commanding healing" method we looked at in the last chapter. The difference is that the Roman officer was willing to believe and exercise his faith in Jesus' word and was confident that Jesus' words of healing would be manifested. Jesus commended the man for exercising such great faith in His words. And then look at what happened.

Then Jesus said to the Roman officer, "Go back home. Because you believed, it has happened." And the young servant was healed that same hour. (Matthew 8:13)

Notice that Jesus said the healing would be delivered because the Roman officer was willing to believe in the power of Jesus' words. And the servant was healed as soon as the officer believed. So using your faith to believe God's word is one way to receive healing. You may wonder how to get faith or how to increase your faith so you can believe for healing like the Roman officer.

So then faith comes by hearing, and hearing by the word of God. (Romans 10:17) (NKJV)

One way to develop your faith is to spend time reading, hearing and speaking God's word. His word is found in the Bible. Realize that God's word is always true and always for our benefit. We all have a choice to either believe or reject anything we read or hear. I encourage you to always believe what you read in the Bible. As you read and hear and believe God's word, your faith increases. God's word reveals who He is. It reveals His character, nature and will. It is the primary way He communicates with us.

"The rain and snow come down from the heavens and stay on the ground to water the earth. They cause the grain to grow, producing seed for the farmer and bread for the hungry. It is the same with my word. I send

it out, and it always produces fruit. It will accomplish all I want it to, and it will prosper everywhere I send it. (Isaiah 55:10–11)

The Spirit alone gives eternal life. Human effort accomplishes nothing. And the very words I have spoken to you are spirit and life. (John 6:63)

For the word of God is alive and powerful.... (Hebrews 4:12)

God's word is like a seed in that it always produces. His word is a spiritual substance which contains the life and power of God. When the seed of the word of God is planted in your spirit and you choose to believe, it will produce what it was sent to produce. God's word on healing will produce healing when we read it or hear it and choose to believe it. That is the kind of faith Jesus praised in the case of the Roman officer and his sick servant.

Believing God's word for healing is something you can do anytime and anywhere. You don't have to be in a church service. You don't have to have a minister with you. You don't have to have your church elders with you. You can do this all on your own. You can choose to exercise your faith and believe that God's healing power is working in you and causing you to be restored to health. I encourage you to use this method whenever you need healing, even if you combine it with one or more of the other methods described in this book. If you ask the elders of your church to pray for you, believe that God's word concerning healing is working in you. If someone lays hands on you for healing, believe that God's word concerning healing is working in you. If you agree with someone in prayer for healing, base your agreement on the word of God concerning healing.

Read God's promises concerning healing. Meditate on those promises. Speak those promises out of your mouth. Remember that His word is alive and powerful. Let His word penetrate into your spirit and cause your physical body to be healed.

Chapter 8: Believing God's Word

My child, pay attention to what I say. Listen carefully to my words. Don't lose sight of them. Let them penetrate deep into your heart, for they bring life to those who find them, and healing to their whole body. (Proverbs 4:20–22)

Many times believing God's word for healing will take time before you see the healing manifested in your body. Unlike the gift of healing, which is usually instantaneous, using your faith in God's word can be a process. It is important to realize that faith operates in the unseen realm. You may not see anything change immediately, but you must keep believing that God's power is at work and things will eventually change for the better.

Faith is the confidence that what we hope for will actually happen; it gives us assurance about things we cannot see. (Hebrews 11:1)

Here are some Scriptures you can stand on to trust God for your healing. These Scriptures reveal that Jesus paid for our healing at the same time He paid for our sins to be forgiven. He shed His blood to pay the penalty for our sins and He took the beating on His back to provide for healing for our bodies. We are saved by our faith and we can also be physically healed by our faith.

Yet it was our weaknesses he carried; it was our sorrows that weighed him down. And we thought his troubles were a punishment from God, a punishment for his own sins! But he was pierced for our rebellion, crushed for our sins. He was beaten so we could be whole. <u>He was whipped so we could be healed</u>. (Isaiah 53:4–5)

That evening many demon-possessed people were brought to Jesus. He cast out the evil spirits with a simple command, and he healed all the sick. This fulfilled the word of the Lord through the prophet Isaiah, who said, "<u>He took our sicknesses and removed our diseases</u>." (Matthew 8:16–17)

He personally carried our sins in his body on the cross so that we can be dead to sin and live for what is right. <u>By his wounds you are healed.</u> (1 Peter 2:24)

I thank God that He is still manifesting healing today when people believe God's word. We should celebrate and thank Him when this method is used to bring healing and restoration to those who are suffering. This is <u>one</u> way that God heals. But it isn't the <u>only</u> way.

Chapter 9
Final Thoughts

This book is about receiving God's supernatural healing. However, I don't want to leave you the impression that healing can only come through supernatural means. God has blessed us with knowledge and wisdom in the area of medical science. We know much more today about the physical body and causes and cures for diseases than any other time in human history. We have also learned how to prevent many diseases through vaccinations and natural means.

For example, decades ago, many people suffered from the crippling disease of polio. But in 1953 a medical doctor named Jonas Salk discovered a vaccine to prevent polio. What an incredible blessing from God! Millions of people were vaccinated and polio was essentially eradicated.

In earlier centuries, people would die from infections that could not be controlled. But now we can take antibiotics for a week and get rid of most infections that at one time could be life-threatening. That is a blessing from God.

Surgery has developed to the point that lives can be saved from traumatic injuries which would have resulted in death in an earlier time. Medicines have been developed to help people overcome a myriad of physical problems.

There is nothing wrong or sinful about getting help from the medical community. You are not demonstrating a lack of faith if you get help from a medical doctor or nutritional specialist who can help your body return to its normal state.

Some sicknesses can be cured by a change to a more healthy diet or adding regular exercise to your life. Nutritional supplements, hormone additions or other natural means can also, at times, help you get well.

Chapter 9: Final Thoughts

Because you believe that God still heals supernaturally today doesn't mean you have to forsake all other means for getting healthy. The important thing is that you understand the difference between what you can do and what God has to do. Some medical problems are beyond anything medical science can help us with. In those cases, we certainly must look to God for His supernatural deliverance. In other cases, we may need to eliminate habits we have developed which cause physical problems. For example, smoking can cause a person to develop cancer, emphysema and other diseases. Eating excessive sugar can cause us to become obese which leads to physical problems like high blood pressure. Sometimes, if we are the cause of the problem, we need to take some steps in the natural realm instead of asking God for a miracle.

The last thing I want to encourage you with is that supernatural healing comes from God. We have a part to play, but ultimately, God is the source. I wish I could tell you that you will always receive healing if you just follow a certain formula. But I can't do that. We will never completely understand why some people receive physical healing while they are still on this earth and others don't.

"The Lord our God has secrets known to no one. We are not accountable for them, but we and our children are accountable forever for all that he has revealed to us, so that we may obey all the terms of these instructions. (Deuteronomy 29:29)

What I can encourage you with is that you should do everything within your power to get well and leave the rest up to God. Start with asking God for help. Do everything you can do with your faith and your believing. If necessary, get help from medical specialists. Follow their directions. And keep believing for God to cause everything to work together for a positive result. Then, if the healing never manifests, at least you will know you did everything you knew to do. The Bible says that, for a Christian, going to heaven is actually a blessing, even if a person would have preferred to stay on earth a little longer.

For to me, living means living for Christ, and dying is even better. But if I live, I can do more fruitful work for Christ. So I really don't know which is better. I'm torn between two desires: I long to go and be with Christ, which would be far better for me. (Philippians 1:21–23)

I thank God that He is still manifesting healing today through many different methods. We should celebrate and thank Him when any method is used to bring healing and restoration to those who are suffering. There are many ways in which God heals, but there is only one healer. His name is JESUS!

About the Author

RANDY CLARK has been teaching the truths of the Bible since graduating from Victory Bible Institute in Tulsa, Oklahoma in 1980.

He has served as a Pastor, Bible School Instructor, Church Planter and Christian Television Station Manager. His ministry has also included a weekly television program and a daily radio outreach.

Randy's ministry travels have taken him across the United States and into foreign countries as close as Canada and Mexico and as far away as Indonesia and Ukraine.

He is the author of numerous books and magazine articles and is the founder of Randy Clark Ministries, a worldwide teaching and training ministry. For more resources from the author visit his website at:

www.RandyClark.info

If this book was a help to you, please go to the Amazon.com listing for the book and leave a review. This will encourage others to take advantage of the information and inspiration found within these pages. This book is also available in Kindle and Audible formats through Amazon.com.

Lightning Source UK Ltd.
Milton Keynes UK
UKHW042252150120
356999UK00015B/2/P

9 781732 424715